Mysteries
of the Sea

Look for other

titles:

Mysteries of the Sea

by Mary Packard

and the Editors of Ripley Entertainment Inc.

illustrations by Ron Zalme

SCHOLASTIC INC.

New York   Toronto   London   Auckland   Sydney
Mexico City   New Delhi   Hong Kong   Buenos Aires

Developed by Nancy Hall, Inc.
Designed by R studio T
Cover design by Atif Toor
Photo research by Sharon Lennon

ISBN 0-439-72563-1

12 11 10 9 8 7 6 5 4 3   5 6 7 8 9 10/0

Printed in the U.S.A.
First printing, April 2005

Contents

Mysteries of the Sea

Introduction

Beneath the Waves

Robert Ripley, creator of Ripley's Believe It or Not!, was the top cartoonist of his time. In his quest to find new and unbelievable stories and facts to fill his newspaper column, Ripley literally went to the ends of the Earth to achieve his goal. During his incredible career, he traveled the equivalent of 19 trips around the globe. Ripley  covered more than 24,000 miles on one journey—8,000 of which were made by ship. It's not surprising then that that the Believe It or Not! archives are chock-full of cartoons that reflect Ripley's fascination with the sea and the marine life that inhabits it.

In *Mysteries of the Sea,* you'll journey down through the five zones of the ocean. At the bottom, you'll get a glimpse of the deep-sea trenches, probably the weirdest, as well as the least explored, places on Earth. The grotesque creatures that make their home on the ocean floor prove Robert Ripley's theory that truth is stranger

than fiction! The undersea chimneys that spew toxic gases from deep inside the Earth and the giant clams and tube worms that thrive beside them could easily have been plucked from the pages of a science fiction novel.

More than 270,000 species of animals are found in the ocean—and marine biologists estimate that there are thousands more yet to be discovered. The Earth's largest animal, as well as creatures that sport built-in lights, and animals that come equipped with their own tiny food factories all swim in the ocean. You'll find whales that sing to each other, cuttlefish that hypnotize their prey, and sharks that devour their siblings before they are even born!

In addition, you'll thrill to the exploits of those who plunge to the depths of the sea in submersibles, like the one named *Alvin* that carried researchers to the wreck of the *Titanic*. You'll also learn how marine life has contributed to medical advances, perhaps one of the most important reasons to protect the sea from pollution. Who knows? Perhaps the cure for cancer lies in the ocean depths.

You can see how much you already know about the ocean by taking the Fathom That! quizzes and Ripley's Brain Buster in each chapter. At the end of the book, try the Pop Quiz and use the handy scorecard to figure out your Ripley's rank. Now take a deep breath. You're about to dive into *Mysteries of the Sea* and discover some of the strangest places and creatures you can imagine.

Believe It!®

CHAPTER 1 Way Down Under

If you think we already know everything there is to know about the ocean, you're in for a big surprise!

Deep Thoughts: Most people think that outer space is the only frontier left to explore. Nothing could be further from the truth! Even though the oceans cover 71 percent of the Earth, we know more about the surface of the moon than we do about the ocean floor—an awesome landscape of plains, volcanoes, mountain ranges, canyons, and deep-sea trenches. Using today's technology, it would take scientists about 125 years just to make an accurate map of it!

Fathom That!

The word fathom, which means "to understand," is also a nautical unit of distance equal to . . .

a. one mile.
b. three feet.
c. six feet.
d. five miles.

Chain, Chain, Chain: Not only is the highest mountain under water, but also the longest mountain range. Consisting of volcanoes averaging more than 14,700 feet in height, the Mid-Ocean Ridge circles the globe, like the seams of a baseball, for more than 31,000 miles.

Tall Peaks: Did you know that the world's highest mountain is not Mount Everest? It's actually Mauna Kea, which measures 31,796 feet from its base on the ocean floor to its peak above Hawaii, beating Mount Everest by 2,761 feet!

Fathom That!

The ocean floor off the East Coast of the United States has been significantly altered by . . .

a. submarines.
b. sea otters digging for clams.
c. oil rigs digging for oil.
d. the mounds that tilefish build to hide themselves from predators.

Breaking New Ground:

Many islands are formed by the action of undersea volcanoes. All it takes is for magma, hot liquid rock from deep inside Earth, to burst through a crack in the ocean floor. The magma, now called lava, brings with it tons of ash, sediment, and mud.

MORE ISLAND COMING SOON!

These build up on the ocean floor as the volcano erupts again and again, until finally, an island bursts through the surface of the sea. A few days after a major eruption in 1957, a brand-new island was born near Faial in the Azore Islands. Eventually, the lava and ash connected it to Faial, adding about a square mile to the island.

New Water View:

Believe It or Not! A new ocean is being formed in Africa right now. A 1,500-mile-long fault line is splitting Africa in two along the Great Rift Valley. As the continent is pulled apart, the valley will drop, and

the ocean will flow into the gap. We won't be singing "Happy Birthday" any time soon, though. The estimated date of the new ocean's birth is millions of years from now.

A Real Meltdown: No one knows for sure where Earth's water came from, but scientists have three theories. About 4.5 billion years ago, Earth was so hot that the planet was a glowing mass of bubbling liquid. One theory is that the hot molten rock gave off steam, which condensed as the planet cooled. Another is that water was contained in the rock and, as the Earth's surface cooled and hardened, the water was released. The third theory is that water was brought by comets that crashed into Earth. Over time, minerals, including salt, seeped from the rock into the oceans, making the salty seawater we know today.

Going Down: If you could take an elevator to the bottom of the sea, you would notice that the ocean is made up of five distinct zones: sunlit, twilight, dark, abyss, and trench. As you go down through each level, the sea changes from the warm, bright blue waters of the sunlit zone to the freezing cold, coal-black waters of the trenches—some of which are deeper than the planet's highest mountain!

SUNLIT

TWILIGHT

DARK

ABYSS

TRENCH

Color-coding:

Many sea creatures are color-coded to blend in with the zone where they live. In the sunlit zone, some fish are dark on top and light on the  bottom. When a predator is above such fish, they blend in with the darker water below. On the other hand, when a predator is below them, the fish are hard to see against the sunlit waters above.

Life Lists:

Earth's oceans are teeming with life. In fact, animals live in all five zones. More than 270,000 species of sea creatures have been named, and new ones are being discovered all the time. In 2000, the Census for Marine Life, a network of scientists from more than 70 countries, began a ten-year project to learn more about life in the oceans. Along the Mid-Atlantic Ridge during just two months in 2004, scientists discovered more than 300 new fish species, 50 new squid and octopus species, and so many microscopic creatures they haven't yet identified them all!

Fathom That!

The difference between an ocean and a sea is that a sea is . . .

a. deeper.
b. not salty.
c. smaller.
d. colder.

Sunny-Side Up:

Most ocean life is found in the sunlit zone, which reaches down to a depth of about 600 feet. This is where dolphins and whales swim, killer whales stalk unwary seals, and penguins and seabirds such as cormorants knife through the water in search of fish. Along the shore, you can see some of this life yourself in tidal pools—miniature oceans where you'll find starfish, anemones, barnacles, mussels, sea urchins, and more.

Bottom of the Food Chain:

The microscopic, single-celled plants that float in the sea are called phytoplankton. They are the primary food source for zooplankton— microscopic animals such as bacteria, larvae, and krill (tiny shrimplike animals). In some places, a single gallon of water can contain thousands of phytoplankton and as many as half a million zooplankton!

Fathom That!

The Sargasso Sea is a two-million-square-mile area of the North Atlantic Ocean filled with . . .

a. oil-bearing silt.
b. thick, abundant, floating seaweed.
c. icebergs.
d. oil spilled from tankers all over the world.

Monster Seaweed:

Giant kelp can grow up to 2 feet per day and reach a height of 175 feet. Kelp forests are found along the open coasts of North and South America, where seawater flows over the kelp's leaflike blades, providing nutrients. Sea creatures live in every part of the forest, from the canopy at the surface to the rootlike holdfasts that anchor the kelp to the ocean floor. Believe It or Not!: Giant kelp forests might not exist if it weren't for sea otters. Why? The otters eat sea urchins, which feed on giant kelp and, if not kept under control, could destroy an entire forest.

Building Big: Australia's Great Barrier Reef is so huge it can be seen from space—yet, like other coral reefs, it was

built from the limestone skeletons of billions and billions of tiny animals called polyps. Teeming with life, coral reefs may support even more kinds of organisms than tropical rain forests.

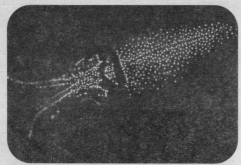

Sun's Gone: Below the sunlit zone lies the twilight zone—yes, that's really what it's called! The twilight zone stretches from about 600 feet to 3,300 feet below the ocean's surface with an average temperature of about 41°F. Light in the twilight zone resembles the light on land at dusk. Some fish spend their days here, but at night swim up to the sunlit zone to feed. Many creatures that live in the twilight zone, such as the three-inch-long firefly squid, sport lights on their bellies and tails.

Living Lights: Real fish don't come with batteries. So how do they make themselves glow in the dark? They don't. Their light comes from bacteria that live inside the fishes' light organs. Bioluminescence, the light shed by the bacteria, is produced by a chemical reaction. These living, breathing night-lights help fish lure prey, attract mates, camouflage their bodies, or temporarily blind their predators—much as a car with blazing headlights blinds oncoming drivers at night.

Slim Pickin's: In the dark zone, which extends from about 3,300 to 13,200 feet below the surface, the water is very cold. There's no sunlight and not much food. That's why many fish, like the gulper eel, have supersized mouths—the better to catch what little nourishment happens to come their way.

How Abyss-mal!

Below the dark zone, the abyssal plains reach a depth of about 19,800 feet. There the still waters are barely above freezing and all is in total darkness. Many of the creatures that live there eat marine snow—the waste and dead bodies of sea animals from the upper layers of the ocean—that covers the ocean floor. Other creatures are clustered near hydrothermal vents, where hot gases bubble up from deep beneath the ocean floor, heating the water.

Fathom That!

Scientists believe that in some places on the ocean floor, marine snow may be as deep as . . .

a. 100 feet.
b. 300 yards.
c. one mile.
d. three miles.

Blackout! Sea trenches can plunge deeper than the tallest mountains rise aboveground. The deepest known spot in the ocean is the Mariana Trench in the western Pacific Ocean, which dips to 35,640 feet below sea level. Trenches are so deep, dark, and cold that few creatures can survive there. Fish bones would be crushed by the pressure caused by thousands of pounds of water pressing down on them. That's why the only living creatures in the trenches are squishy boneless animals, such as microbes, shrimp, sea cucumbers, and worms. Most of these creatures are blind since, without light, eyes are useless.

Double Agents: Unlike many fish that travel through the upper levels of the sea in large groups called schools, deep-sea creatures don't have a lot of company. There is less food to eat, so there are fewer animals—so few that certain kinds have trouble finding mates. That's why some of these animals, including deep-sea anglerfish and tripod fish, are hermaphrodites—organisms that are male and female at the same time and can reproduce themselves!

What's Up? Gravity holds the ocean to the Earth. However, the level of the ocean rises and falls twice each day. That's because the sun and the moon—especially the moon, which is closer—pull on the water like two giant magnets, creating high and low tides. The highest and lowest tides occur twice a month when the sun, moon, and Earth are directly in line.

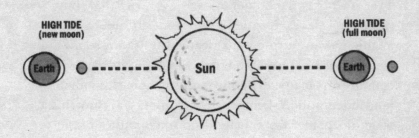

HIGH TIDE (new moon) — Earth — Sun — Earth — HIGH TIDE (full moon)

Extreme Tidings: The highest tides on Earth occur in the Bay of Fundy in Canada, where the tides rise and fall an average of 52.5 feet—twice a day! The tides that surge up the narrowing River Severn in England regularly reach 50 feet near the town of Chepstow, and one tide was recorded as reaching 70 feet!

Fathom That!

The Arctic Sea is the world's . . .

a. shallowest ocean.
b. deepest ocean.
c. saltiest ocean.
d. biggest ocean.

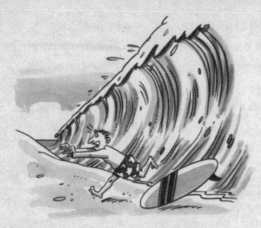

Walls of Water: Most of the waves in the ocean are caused by the wind. The highest wind-caused wave was recorded in 1933. While crossing the Pacific Ocean during a hurricane, the USS *Ramapo* reported a 112-foot-high wave. Tsunamis are waves caused by volcanic eruptions, undersea earthquakes, landslides, and avalanches. In the open sea, tsunamis are wide, deep, and fast moving—up to 600 miles per hour—but not very high. As they reach the shallower waters near land, they slow slightly but gain in height. When tsunamis rush ashore, the first wave may reach almost a hundred feet, destroying everything in its wake.

Ocean in Motion: Did you know that there are rivers in the ocean called currents? The main forces that produce currents are the sun's heat, the winds pushing on the surface of the water, gravity, and the Earth's rotation. Currents can have a huge effect on the weather on land. For example, the Gulf Stream carries warm water from the Caribbean Sea up the eastern coast of the United States and across the Atlantic Ocean to England and northern Europe. Without the Gulf Stream, these parts of the world would be a lot colder.

Ship to Shore: There is enough stuff floating in the ocean to fill several shopping malls. Each year, more than 10,000 containers fall off of storm-tossed ships, spilling their cargo into the sea. For instance, in 1990, 80,000 sneakers went overboard and in 2000, millions of Lego pieces were lost. As long as it floats, the cargo may circle the globe for years before it washes up on the shore. So next time you go to the beach, keep your eye out—you may find a real bargain!

Weathering the Sea: The oceans are responsible for some of the world's worst weather, including hurricanes (in some places called typhoons and cyclones), severe rainstorms called monsoons, and dense sea fog.

Fathom That!

In 1958, an earthquake caused a landslide in an enclosed inlet near Juneau, Alaska, resulting in a wave that reached . . .

a. 150 feet high.
b. 980 feet high.
c. 1,720 feet high.
d. one mile high.

Raining Sprats and Frogs: In August 2000, rain dropped more than just water on a seacoast town in England. The citizens of Great Yarmouth stepped outside to find their lawns covered with fish called sprats! What caused it? A tornado-like funnel of air called a waterspout. Waterspouts form over the ocean, sucking up water and anything that's in it. It whirls through the air until it finally loses steam and drops its load. Things could have been worse. The Ripley archives are full of reports of towns around the world being pelted with birds, fish, turtles, and even maggots. Yuck!

Fathom That!

In 1997, a waterspout arose near the Mexican town of Villa Angel Flores and dumped a rain of . . .

a. dead snakes.
b. guppies.
c. mussels.
d. live toads.

Time to get your feet wet. See if you can tell the difference between what's true blue and what's so false it will blow you out of the water!

Robert Ripley dedicated his life to seeking out the bizarre and unusual, but every unbelievable thing he recorded was proven to be true. In the Brain Buster at the end of every chapter, you'll play Ripley's role—trying to verify the fantastic facts presented. Each Ripley's Brain Buster contains a group of four shocking statements. Of these so-called "facts," **one** is **fiction**. Will you **Believe It!** or **Not!**?

Wait! there's more! Following the Brain Busters are special bonus questions where you can earn extra points! Keep score by flipping to the end of the book for the answer key and a scorecard.

Three of the following sea stories are buoyed by the truth. Plumb the depth of your knowledge about the ocean and see if you can spot the falsehood that won't hold water.

a. If all the salt were extracted from the ocean, it would form a five-foot-deep blanket across the world's seven continents.

b. Scientists have identified a giant wave circling Antarctica, which is as large as the continent of Australia and almost a mile deep.

c. Waterspouts cause more damage than tornadoes and hurricanes put together.

d. There is really just one huge ocean on Earth, even though we have divided it into the Atlantic, Pacific, Indian, Antarctic, and Arctic Oceans.

• •

BONUS GAME

People don't usually think of the ocean as freezing, but of course it does. When ice forms in the ocean, it leaves behind most of its salt content. There are many names for the different types of ice floating in the sea. See how many you can match to their descriptions.

1. Icebergs

a. Small icebergs about the size of a house

2. Pancake ice

b. Long slicks of ice

3. Grease ice

c. Round pieces of freezing slush

4. Bergy bits

d. Huge blocks of ice that have broken off glaciers

Whether warm-blooded or cold-blooded, many of the largest creatures in the world are not found on land, but in the ocean.

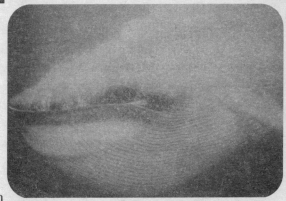

Toothless Giant: The largest animal in the world, the blue whale grows more than 100 feet in length and weighs up to 130 tons—as heavy as 30 full-grown elephants! Instead of teeth, it has as many as 800 two- to twenty-foot-long fringed plates called baleen hanging from its upper jaw that filter the krill that it eats from seawater. It takes four tons of krill a day to fill the belly of one adult blue whale!

Fathom That!

The tongue of a blue whale is as long as a . . .

a. school bus.
b. compact car.
c. tugboat.
d. bicycle.

Into the Breach:
Some scientists think that whales breach, or launch themselves out of the water in spectacular jumps, not only to shake off parasites but also to show off to other whales and just have fun!

Wolves of the Sea: Even though they are really members of the dolphin family, orcas are called killer whales because they are such skilled hunters. Each day, they scoop up hundreds of pounds of seafood made

up of a smorgasbord of fish, sea lions, birds, and even other whales. Extremely social animals, orcas often hunt in pods, groups of between 5 and 30 whales. Each pod is led by a female orca. Many experts think that orcas talk to each other in a complex language that differs from pod to pod.

Tuned In: In 1985, when a sudden Arctic freeze blocked their only passage back to the open sea, about 3,000 white beluga whales were trapped in small

pools in the ice. A Soviet icebreaker was able to ram through the ice to create a pathway for the whales to escape. However, it was not until classical music was piped through the ship's speakers that the whales were enticed to follow the boat to safety.

Spouting Off: Beluga whales are nicknamed "sea canaries" because they are so vocal. In a study of belugas conducted by Russian scientists, the whales were found to have unique voices that varied in pitch from soprano to bass. The researchers expect that they will soon be able to distinguish one whale from another not only by the way it looks but also by its unique voice!

Fathom That!

Although whales are completely at home in the water, they are mammals and have to come up to the surface of the water to breathe at least . . .

a. once every two hours.
b. twice a day.
c. once every 15 minutes.
d. once an hour.

Broken Records:

The songs of male humpback whales are made up of a complicated series of clicks, low moans, and high squeals. They have been known to last 30 minutes, then start all over again with all the same clicks, moans, and squeals—in the exact same order! More amazing still, all humpbacks of the same region will sing the same song, but that song will differ from songs sung by humpbacks living elsewhere.

Boom Boxes:
Whales produce the sounds they make by circulating air inside a nasal cavity in front of their blowholes. In sperm whales, this sound system can actually be seen as a large bulbous shape on their foreheads. The male humpback whale's song is so loud that if you were to swim beside a singing whale you would feel your whole body vibrate!

Here I Am! Why do whales sing? Scientists know that whales are highly intelligent animals that form close bonds with other whales of their species. They think that whale songs can be compared to the bright plumage displayed by male birds to attract mates.

They may also be singing to let their companions know where they are and what they are up to. Scientists believe that some whales' songs can be detected by other whales from hundreds and maybe thousands of miles away!

Haunting Music: The haunting songs of the whales were first heard long ago by seamen who thought they were hearing the ghosts of drowned sailors. Today, the strangely beautiful underwater music of whales is so widely appreciated that recordings of their songs are actually sold in record stores around the world!

Fathom That!

In its 70-year lifetime, a single sperm whale might . . .

a. travel around the entire Earth.
b. consume enough fish to fill an Olympic-sized swimming pool.
c. learn 100 different songs.
d. give birth to 1,000 babies.

Heavy Hitter:
Male, or bull, sperm whales are the largest toothed whales, growing up to 59 feet long. They are also extremely fierce predators. Their teeth can grow up to six inches long, and each one weighs half a pound! Bull sperm whales use their massive, blunt heads as battering rams against anything in their path—including ships. In 1902, the whaling ship *Kathleen* was attacked by a bull sperm whale and sank in 20 minutes!

Giants of the Sea:
Of all the creatures in the sea, the giant squid is perhaps the most mysterious. That's because no one has ever captured a full-grown giant squid alive. Based on the size of remains found on the shore and in the sea, scientists estimate that these giants can weigh several tons and reach up to 100 feet in length. What *is* certain is that the giant squid is the largest invertebrate (animal without a backbone) in the world.

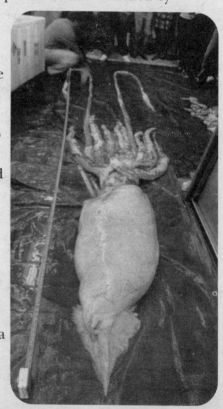

Scar Face: Sperm whales and giant squid are deadly enemies, each regarding the other as a potential meal. How do we know? Scientists have found giant

squid meat in dead sperm whales and sperm whale meat inside the belly of a dead giant squid that washed up on shore. In a fight, a giant squid and a sperm whale are pretty evenly matched. Even if the whale wins, however, it won't get away unharmed. In fact, most sperm whales bear the battle scars of their fights—telltale circular marks made by the suckers at the ends of a squid's tentacles.

Get a Grip! The giant squid has eyes the size of dinner plates, making it unlikely that any prey would escape its notice. Its arsenal of weapons include a razor-sharp beak that can slice through steel cable, and eight arms, each up to 17 feet long and lined with hundreds of suckers containing tiny teeth. It also has two tentacles, each as long as 33 feet, which have suckers at the end. Once a giant squid grabs onto something, it won't have an easy time getting away!

Armed and Dangerous!

Based on an incident said to have occurred on May 10, 1874, it may be a good thing that humans and giant squid have had so little contact. Apparently, a giant squid attacked and sank a 150-ton schooner named *Pearl*. The giant squid may also be the legendary kraken, a sea monster said to attack sailing ships and pull them under with its long arms.

Technicolor Terrors: The giant cuttlefish can grow up to six feet in length. Cuttlefish are masters of disguise, changing color patterns in a shimmer of red, reddish-brown, gold, silver, and white as they swim. Other cuttlefish know exactly what each pattern means. One might say, "Stay away!" Another might say, "I'm looking for a mate." Sometimes cuttlefish use color changes to hypnotize their prey. At other times they use them to blend in with their surroundings as they hide from predators or wait to ambush an unsuspecting morsel.

Real-Life Jaws:

In September 2004, a 14-foot-long, 1,750-pound female great white shark became trapped in a bay off the coast of Cape Cod, Massachusetts. In order to follow her for research

purposes, scientists placed an electronic tracking device on her dorsal fin. It is extremely rare for a great white shark to drift so close to land and to stay for more than a week. Sightseers were advised not to get too close, however, since a great white's jaws are lined with some 3,000 very sharp, jagged teeth!

Tooth Factories:

Sharks never have to worry about losing a tooth. That's because their mouths are like little tooth factories with an ever-ready supply of replacements. Shark teeth grow in five rows. When a front tooth breaks or falls out, it is replaced by another tooth in the row behind it. The spare teeth rotate forward and a new one starts growing in the back.

Fathom That!

Which of the following facts is not true? Great white sharks . . .

a. are very social animals that usually travel in pods.
b. have no bones.
c. do not chew their prey.
d. have to keep swimming all the time in order to breathe.

Supersensitive: The black dots visible on a shark's snout aren't zits. They're actually a secret weapon called ampullae of Lorenzini. Clear gel inside a network of pores in a shark's snout helps it to sense when a fish is near by detecting its weak magnetic field. Recently, scientists have begun to think these pores also act as a sensitive thermometer, able to pick up changes in water temperature as small as a thousandth of a degree.

A Whale of a Shark: The whale shark grows to about 40 feet long and has a mouth so big you can look into it

and see out through its gills! Not to worry if you run into one, however. Whale sharks are filter feeders, swimming along with their mouths wide open to take in plankton, sardines, and other small fish.

Tooling Along: Hammerhead sharks are possibly the strangest looking sharks in the ocean. Their wide heads, however, give them the advantage of an extra-large area for their ampullae of Lorenzini. The eyes of the great hammerhead shark are three feet apart. Like other hammerhead sharks, it has good side vision but can't see directly in front of it. A great hammerhead can start munching on a stingray from the outside edge of the wing while still holding the stingray pinned to the ocean floor with one side of its head.

Sibling Nibling: Some sharks bear live young instead of laying eggs. In some species, such as the thresher shark and the sand tiger shark, the young that hatch first gobble up their own brothers and sisters!

Fathom That!

Unlike most fish, hammerhead and tiger sharks have . . .

a. lungs.
b. eyelids.
c. eyelashes.
d. claws.

Super Star: The crown of thorns starfish can grow to be almost three feet in diameter and have up to 21 arms covered with two-inch-long spines. They live in the Great Barrier Reef off Australia and gobble up coral, sometimes faster than the coral can replace itself.

Grand Clam: Clammers don't often come across giant clams. If they did, they'd have to build a huge bonfire for their clambake. People who hunt for clams usually find their hauls in the coastal seas and not on the coral reefs where giant clams make their home. These immense shellfish can weigh over five hundred pounds and reach a length of more than four feet. One reason they grow so big is because, like many corals, they have plant cells that convert sunlight, water, and carbon dioxide into nutrients within their own bodies.

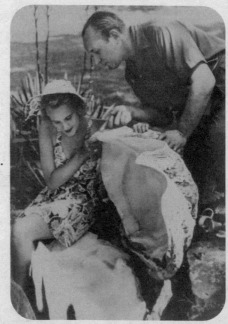

Diamonds in the Rough: Manta rays can grow up to 29.5 feet wide and weigh as much as 3,000 pounds. Yet they are among the most graceful of all sea creatures. Diamond-shaped, they flap their winglike fins as they swim and seem to fly through the water. Manta rays will often leap seven feet into the air, only to smack down again—it's the best way to shake off pesky parasites that have attached themselves to their skin.

The Big Sting: Manta rays are gentle giants, but electric torpedo rays can give shocks and stingrays have venomous spines. Stingrays often bury themselves in the sand to wait for dinner to find them. That's why swimmers and divers have to be especially careful. Stepping on one can result in serious injury!

Fathom That!

Every year, a female crown of thorns starfish can produce as many as a . . .

a. thousand eggs.
b. million eggs.
c. hundred million eggs.
d. billion eggs.

Surprise! In 1938, South African fishermen caught a five-foot-long fish that had a large head and was covered with oddly shaped blue scales. Unable to identify the fish, Marjorie Courtenay-Latimer, curator of the East London Museum in South Africa, had it preserved and sent a sketch of it to James L. B. Smith, a chemistry professor at Rhodes University in Grahamstown and an expert on fish. Smith couldn't believe his eyes. As soon as he could get away, he traveled to East London to see the preserved fish and there was no doubt about it: He was looking at a coelacanth, a creature thought to have become extinct more than 65 million years before!

Fathom That!

People who live on the Comoro Islands use the scales of the coelacanth . . .

a. for sandpaper.
b. to make jewelry.
c. to make cement.
d. for fertilizer.

The ocean is populated by some mighty big—and big-brained—sea creatures, but only you can go fishing for the truth. Can you tell which three fish stories are true and which one is a whale of a whopper?

a. Twice a year, natives of the Fiji Islands take part in a ritual in which they pull sharks from their nets with their bare hands, then turn them over and kiss their bellies.

b. The oarfish is the longest bony fish, reportedly growing up to 56 feet long.

c. The beaked whale is so rare that in the last 25 years, scientists have found only three complete specimens to confirm that it even exists.

d. In Hawaii, jellyfish are getting scarce because the latest fashion trend is to dry them out and use them for pendants, brooches, and hair ornaments.

BONUS GAME

What kind of sea creature is often a home for other sea creatures, can grow so big that a diver could stand inside it with room to spare, and can live underwater for hundreds of years?

_ _ _ _ _   _ _ _ _ _ _   _ _ _ _ _ _

CHAPTER 3 Sea-riously Strange!

So what's going on below while you're treading water in the ocean? You'd be surprised!

Hard of Herring: Just because herrings can't talk doesn't mean they can't communicate. Researchers studying captive herring heard a fast, repetitive, tick, tick, tick, or FRT for short. It was the sound fish make when they pass gas! The herring do this at night when it's dark. The researchers think that the FRT sounds herring make are a code to let others in their group know where they are and what they are doing!

Fathom That!

The moon snail eats a clam . . .

a. by dissolving the clam's shell with its acidlike saliva.
b. by smashing it against a rock.
c. from the inside out after darting inside the clam when its shell is open.
d. by drilling a hole in the clam's shell with its tongue.

Class Action: Many types of fish hang out together in crowds called schools. A school of fish is one of nature's wonders—the school can speed up, slow down, or hang a U-turn with such precision, it's as if the fish were all governed by one brain! How do they do it? Fish have tiny sense organs all along their bodies that give them a sixth sense. This is called the "lateral line system" or "sense of distant touch." It allows individual fish to detect even minute vibrations in the water, which in turn, allows the school of fish to move as one body.

Taillight: The light-producing organ at the end of the gulper eel's tail flashes red, so when it whips its tail into position near its head, the light attracts fish into its enormous waiting jaws.

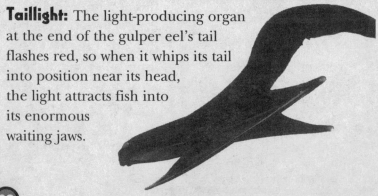

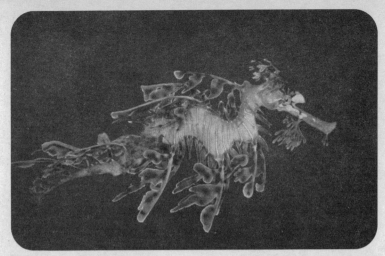

Hiding in Plain Sight: The leafy seadragon of Australia is often mistaken for drifting seaweed—until it sucks its prey into its snout like a vacuum cleaner.

Seeing-Eye Fish: The pistol shrimp has poor eyesight, so a fish called Luther's watchman goby stands guard and warns the shrimp of danger while it digs an underwater burrow for both species to share.

Sole Food—Not! The Moses sole, a fish found in the Red Sea, can repel sharks by secreting a poison that works on the sharks' gills, preventing them from getting oxygen. The sharks have to swim away to force clear water through their gills and get rid of the poison.

Fathom That!

Gulper eels can swallow prey . . .

a. only after it's been well chewed.
b. that is full of venom.
c. that is twice their size.
d. that is the same size as they are.

Time for a Change: All sand crabs are male for the first two years of their lives. During that time, they mate with older female crabs. However, when the males turn two, they suddenly change gender, become female, and begin laying eggs!

Brilliant Bones: Coral reefs are actually the skeletons of polyps, tiny soft-bodied sea creatures that live in warm, shallow water. Polyps get their brilliant colors from the algae that live inside them. Algae are plants that use the sun's energy to make food. During the daylight hours, it's the algae that help the coral reef grow.

Fathom That!

A lot of the muscles in the suckers of the Stauroteuthis syrtensis, an orange-colored deep-sea octopus, have been replaced by . . .

a. little webbed feet.
b. light-emitting organs.
c. strong claws.
d. venom glands.

Covering All Bases: Coral polyps will attach themselves to almost anything—rocks, the skeletons of dead animals, whatever's around. Even an airplane that has crashed into the sea can serve as a canvas for a coral creation!

Hiding in Plain Sight: Many sea animals that live in coral reefs use camouflage to protect themselves from predators or to conceal themselves from potential prey. The purple stonefish, for example, looks more like the coral it lives in than like a fish. The red windowpane-plaid markings on the hawkfish help conceal it as it swims among red-branched coral. Some creatures, such as bubble coral shrimp, don't need camouflage— instead, they are almost entirely transparent.

Blood Brothers: Did you know that a type of snail called the vampire snail crawls from its hiding place in the sandy seabed at night to suck the blood of sleeping fish?

Slime Time: The front teeth of the parrotfish have fused together to form the parrotlike beak that gives the fish its name. It uses the beak to scrape algae from the coral reef—and sometimes the coral itself—which it then grinds up with molarlike teeth in its throat. Soon after dark, parrotfish wrap themselves in see-through "blankets" made out of mucus. The fish produce the mucus in their mouths and pass it backward in thick folds. This prevents predators—though not the vampire snail—from smelling the fish while it sleeps.

Trigger Happy: A triggerfish has two dorsal fins on its back. The front fin usually lies in a groove along the fish's back. To keep itself safe at night, the triggerfish finds a good hiding place, then raises the first fin, snaps together the first two spines inside, and sticks the now rigid fin up into the rock or coral to lock itself in place.

Fathom That!

The mere sight of a trumpet fish sends its fishy prey swimming for cover, so to catch a meal, it . . .

a. hitches a ride on a parrotfish.
b. swims backward toward its prey.
c. always attacks from behind.
d. carries seaweed in its mouth for camouflage.

Good Grooming: There's nothing a cleaner wrasse likes better than a mouthful of parasites. These fish set up shop

in special areas of the coral reef where larger fish, such as the giant moray eel, come to let the wrasses rid them of annoying pests. Wrasses will even pick the parasites from between a fish's teeth!

The Cod Father: The National Marine Fisheries Service, along with Oregon State University, has developed a "classroom" where baby salmon learn how to avoid the predatory codfish. The cod are placed in a

large tank, inside of which is a smaller salmon tank. By watching how the cod try to attack them, the salmon learn how to dodge their main predator.

The Terminator:

Mantis shrimp may be called shrimp, but they are really only distant relatives. These vicious predators can grow to be up to a foot long. Some species of mantis shrimp have razor-sharp claws that resemble a switchblade and can slice a fish in two—or cut a human hand to the bone—in less than a second. Other species have a club-shaped front leg that they use to smash open the shells of snails. In April 2004, researchers filmed a peacock mantis shrimp repeatedly hitting a tegula snail with its club and were able to measure the incredible speed and force it used.

Nice Trick! The *Linckia columbiae* species of starfish can regrow its entire body from a single severed piece of itself measuring less than half an inch in length!

Fathom That!

The *Phronima sedentaria* shrimp lays its eggs in the hollowed-out body of a sea organism called a salp, then . . .

a. swims away and never sees the eggs again.
b. covers the salp with sand.
c. pushes the salp around like a baby carriage until the young have hatched.
d. hides the salp in a coral reef.

Strong Stomach: The starfish has the bizarre ability to capture and eat prey by turning its stomach inside out and thrusting it out through its mouth!

On the Move: Spiny lobsters are clawless lobsters that can grow up to two feet long and have shells covered with sharp spines. Every year, these creatures migrate long distances across the ocean floor, walking in single file. Each spiny lobster uses its antennae to maintain contact with the lobster in front of it, and the leader of the line changes often. If threatened, the lobsters don't stop moving but stick out their long antennae toward the intruder, as if saying "Keep your distance!"

Big Mama:
Though the female blanket octopus can grow to be more than 6 feet long, the male doesn't get longer than two-thirds of an inch! Blanket

octopuses are immune to the sting of the Portuguese man-of-war and have been known to rip off the jellyfish's tentacles and use them to defend themselves against predators!

Lid Flipper: You may be surprised to find out how smart an octopus named Frieda is. Her caretakers at a zoo in Munich, Germany, certainly were! After watching her keepers twist open the lids of jars containing her food,

Frieda learned how to open a jar all by herself. Now she opens jars all the time. She won't open just any jar, though—only the ones containing such special treats as shrimp, clams, and crabs. Yum!

Box of Poison: The hawksbill turtle is able to swallow the box jellyfish, or sea wasp, found in the waters off Australia, despite the fact that this jellyfish is considered among the most venomous animals on Earth. One sting is so deadly, it can kill a human in four minutes, yet the hawksbill turtle is never harmed in the slightest!

Jelly Poppins: A striped jellyfish propels itself through the water by expanding and contracting its top like an umbrella. When it expands, it sucks in water, when it contracts, it squeezes the water out the back like a jet engine and the jellyfish shoots forward. Squid, octopuses, and cuttlefish contract their muscular bodies to get around in much the same way.

Fathom That!

A jellyfish is 95 percent . . .

a. gas.
b. mucus.
c. water.
d. salt.

Getting Slugged!

Red gilled nudibranches are actually sea slugs. Instead of having gills, these strange-looking creatures breathe through their skin. The long, red, white-tipped tubes called cerata on its back provide extra skin to take in more air. The cerata also have stinging cells. Where do they come from? These amazing creatures actually eat the stinging cells of anemones, which then move through their bodies to the tips of the cerata.

Wee Horse: Scientists at McGill University in Montreal, Canada, have just made an amazing discovery in the Flores Sea off the coast of Indonesia—a new species of seahorse so small it could fit inside a thimble! Given that it's just over a half-inch from its nose to the tip of its tail, it's no wonder this tiny seahorse was able to stay hidden for so long!

Fathom That!

The three-inch-long *Heteroteuthis dispar* squid defends itself from enemies by . . .

a. releasing a cloud of glowing, bioluminescent ink to blind them.
b. spitting poisonous venom at them.
c. beating them with its arms.
d. biting them with its sharp beak.

By now, you know just how strange many sea creatures really are. The question is can you tell which three of the statements below are fact and which one is simply fishy?

a. The crimson medusa jellyfish, a delicacy served at special occasions in Japan, tastes very similar to strawberry jam.

b. The giant Japanese spider crab can develop a leg span of up to 12 feet.

c. Seahorses mate for life. The female seahorse deposits her eggs in a male seahorse's pouch, and he gives birth to the babies.

d. Mantis shrimp have been known to break the glass of aquariums.

BONUS GAME

Salps live in colonies in the open ocean and swim by jet propulsion. They are usually transparent but produce bright light just like a chemical light stick. These strange creatures can attach themselves to each other, forming chains up to 33 feet long. In early times, sailors often mistook these long chains of salps for . . .

— — —   — — — — — — — —

CHAPTER 4
Gifts from the Sea

Besides food, many other types of treasures can be found in the deep blue seas.

Carra-what? Read the labels on a carton of ice cream, a bottle of salad dressing, a jar of peanut butter, and on lots of other products, and chances are you'll find an ingredient called carrageenan. Found in seaweed, carrageenan is used as a thickener. It's what keeps peanut butter creamy and prevents it from separating from its natural oils. It also makes marshmallows gooey and gives ice cream its wonderful, smooth texture.

Fathom That!

The Ainu people of Japan use salmon skin to make . . .

a. boots.
b. canoes.
c. sunscreen.
d. cradles for their babies.

Fishy Locks:

Dr. Robert Hoffman of Maine has developed a method of making human hair grow green, blue, yellow, or red by using genes taken from tropical fish. Now if  he could just get it to grow on bald people!

Eau d'Intestine: A waxy gray substance called ambergris is the base of many very expensive perfumes. Believe It or Not!, ambergris is found in one place, and one place only—the large intestines of sperm whales!

Sponge Power: In laboratory tests on mice, scientists discovered that compounds extracted from a deep-sea sponge found in the Indian and Pacific Oceans were very effective in fighting malaria and may possibly work against tuberculosis and AIDS as well.

Snail Meds: The marine cone snail has a hollow tooth with a harpoonlike barb at the end. When it detects prey, it sticks out its tooth, called a radula, and uses it to stab, inject paralyzing venom, and reel in its next meal. The cone snail's venom is poisonous enough to kill a human within minutes—yet researchers believe the venom holds the key to relieving chronic pain. Scientists have created a synthetic version of the cone snail's venom that is 1,000 times stronger than morphine. Called Ziconotide, it kills pain effectively and has no side effects. Currently, Ziconotide is in its third phase of clinical testing and may soon be helping thousands of people with arthritis, cancer, and other painful diseases.

Fathom That!

British scientists have found a substance in shrimp that they are using to make . . .

a. nasal spray for allergy sufferers.
b. foot powder.
c. ear drops.
d. mosquito repellent.

Fish Breath: Dr. John Smart of the University of Portsmouth in England designed a bacteria-fighting toothpaste from crab shells.

Wishing on Stars: Research scientists are experimenting with using starfish to repair the damaged jaws of cancer patients and accident victims. Although bone transplants are often rejected, they're hoping that starfish skeletons will not be.

An Open Book: Clams only live for about 20 years, but their empty shells endure for hundreds of years in the ocean. When sliced open by paleontologists, the formation of the shells can provide clues to the temperature and contents of ancient seas.

Fathom That!

The melo melo snail found in waters off Vietnam produces . . .

a. slime that's used in hair gel.
b. a substance used in finger paints.
c. rare, bright orange pearls.
d. a chemical used in lipstick.

Putting Some Mussel into It:

Mussels excrete threads covered with a sticky substance that is so tough it holds the shells firmly to their perches—even when they're being pounded by the heavy surf. Today, research scientists are experimenting with ways to use the gluey substance to bond human bones and save human teeth.

Thick-Skinned:

The skin of the gar fish is so strong that Native Americans once used it as a protective breastplate, and they used its scales to make arrows.

Totally Shark-ing!

In Iceland, hakarl is considered a local delicacy. What is it? Rotten shark. To make it, large chunks of cut-up shark are buried in the sand where they'll be covered by the high tide. After about eight weeks, the chunks are dug out and strung up to dry for another eight or so weeks. Then they're cut into pices and served with ice-cold Brennevin, a caraway-flavored liquor also called "black death."

Nice Catch! Growing up to 12 feet long and weighing more than 1,500 pounds, the Atlantic blue-fin tuna is valued as food and as a game fish. In fact, it may be the most valuable fish in the world. In 2002, a single tuna sold for 250,000 dollars in Tokyo, Japan.

Living Fossils

Out of the Blue: In 1938, scientists were amazed when South African fishermen caught a blue, five-foot-long coelacanth—a fish that was thought to have been extinct for at least 60 million years.

Big Snout: First caught in 1897 by Japanese fishermen off the coast of Yokohama, the rare goblin shark is a throwback to sharks that lived 25 to 30 million years ago. With its dagger-shaped snout, it could not look more prehistoric!

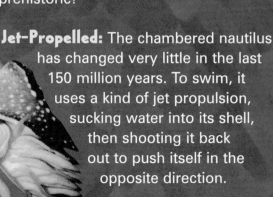

Jet-Propelled: The chambered nautilus has changed very little in the last 150 million years. To swim, it uses a kind of jet propulsion, sucking water into its shell, then shooting it back out to push itself in the opposite direction.

Fooled Ya!
The 24-inch-long mimic octopus can discourage predators by changing its form to resemble poisonous creatures such as the lionfish and the banded sea snake.

Not Clowning Around!

Unlike other fish, clownfish are immune to the sting of anemones, whose poisonous tentacles make the perfect haven for a clownfish on the run from predators.

Hot Tip: Stay away from the fire urchin—or you'll find out how it got its name! This sea urchin's spines have bulbous tips filled with venom that cause a fiery sensation if touched. Small shrimp often live among the spines for protection.

Defense

Gulp! When threatened, the porcupine fish gulps down water until it balloons into a ball of sharp spines, making it impossible for a predator to swallow.

How Stunning! The cuttlefish changes color at will for a variety of reasons, one of which is to hypnotize its prey!

Sand Trap: Sand diver lizardfish bury themselves in the sand, both to hide from predators and to ambush any unwary prey that may wander by.

The

Turned On: Flashlight fish are equipped with glowing pockets of bacteria below their eyes, which help while hunting in dark water. When a predator is around, however, they can raise a special flap of skin to hide their light and prevent themselves from being seen.

Hiding in Plain Sight: Only a few parts of the *Lycoteuthis* squid are not transparent— and they are hidden by light organs, which break up the squid's silhouette, making it hard to detect by predators and prey.

Lightheaded: The female anglerfish doesn't have to hunt for her meals. She simply relies on the bulblike lure filled with light-producing bacteria on the top of her head to attract fish for dinner.

Twilight Zone

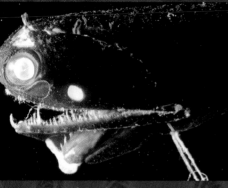

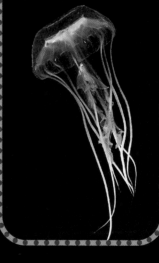

Brilliant Blobs of Light: When a crowd of luminous jellyfish get together, they glow so brightly that they can light up the dark sea for miles.

Red Light, Green Light: The stoplight loosejaw fish has red and green light pockets near its eyes and loosely hinged jaws that are longer than its skull.

Lights Out: The deep-sea shrimp can emit a cloud of light to temporarily blind or distract a predator, allowing the shrimp to disappear into the dark water.

Beauties . . .

Fairest of Them All: When it comes to natural beauties, none are lovelier than fairy basslets, which make their home among the coral reefs.

Top Notch: The jeweled-top snail would not look out of place in a jewelry box, but the place to find it is in the kelp forest in Monterey Bay, California. Tucked inside its shell are tentacles that the snail uses for smelling and touching.

Hidden Beauty: Brightly colored *Tubastraea,* or cup corals, live in shady places and feed on microscopic sea creatures.

... and the Beasts

Muppet Man: No wonder the red-spotted blenny spends so much time hidden inside its coral home. If you looked like a Muppet with measles, you'd probably hide, too.

R-eel Tame: Despite its unfortunate face, the wolf eel is a charming fellow. Though their sharp teeth and powerful jaws are good for crunching sea urchins, wolf eels have been known to take food gently from the hands of divers.

Batty Looking: Only a mother could love the ugly batfish, which uses its fins to crawl along the ocean floor.

Low Lives

Deep Thoughts: In 1979, *Alvin*, the world's first deep-sea submersible, gave scientists their first glimpse of geothermal vents, which are called smokers, and the strange sea life that thrives around them.

Smokin'! Geothermal vents (below) blast out hot dark fluids filled with minerals and poisonous gases, such as hydrogen sulfide. Bacteria that live on hydrogen sulfide support entire ecosystems of larger sea creatures.

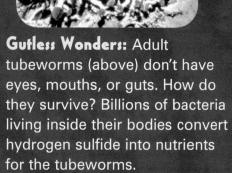

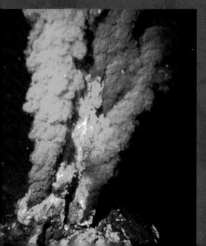

Gutless Wonders: Adult tubeworms (above) don't have eyes, mouths, or guts. How do they survive? Billions of bacteria living inside their bodies convert hydrogen sulfide into nutrients for the tubeworms.

Something's Fishy:

The deep-sea oarfish helps Japanese scientists predict earthquakes. Oarfish usually live over 650 feet below sea level, so as soon as they're spotted swimming near the surface of the water, scientists know from past experience that an earthquake is sure to follow.

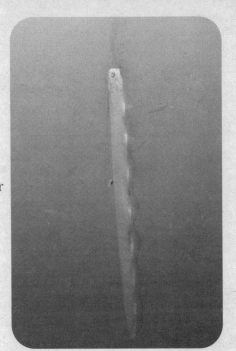

Slime Cure: The Arabian saltwater catfish secretes a slime on its outer skin containing some 60 proteins that can help heal human and animal wounds rapidly.

Fathom That!

Though it's too expensive to remove, the seafloor contains an abundant supply of . . .

a. wood.
b. coal.
c. emeralds.
d. diamonds.

In Cold Blood:

Scientists in Boulder, Colorado, have discovered that blood from a fish in Antarctica contains chemicals that can keep ice cream and other frozen foods from thawing.

Prince of Snails: The deep rich purple that has come to symbolize the color of royalty in some cultures comes from a dye derived from a gland of the marine snail, *Murex brandaris*. The extract was so valued in the Roman Empire that it was worth its weight in gold.

Eye-deal: In 1992, doctors at the University of South Florida began using coral to replace human bone in reconstructive surgery. Certain corals obtained in the South Pacific are perfect for making artificial eyes.

Fathom That!

Scientists use the blue blood of horseshoe crabs to . . .

a. bind dentures to toothless gums.
b. color specimen slides.
c. test medicine for bacteria.
d. bind together the ingredients in vitamin pills.

Brain Buster

If we take good care of our oceans, they will continue to supply us with an endless array of resources. Below are three seaworthy statements about the kinds of natural resources we get from the ocean. Can you deep-six the one statement that is total fiction?

a. Though America's first settlers used lobsters to fertilize their gardens and to feed to prisoners, they never ate lobster meat themselves.

b. Researchers have devised a way to use dead jellyfish as packing material in place of Bubble Wrap, which is not biodegradable.

c. Because zebrafish have the unique ability to regenerate heart muscle tissue, scientists are studying them in the hope of gaining a better understanding of how to heal human hearts.

d. In 1933, Carol Joan Farol of New Orleans found 106 pearls in one oyster.

BONUS GAME

When the mussel population began to dwindle in the sea off the coast of Delaware, marine biologists knew they would have to create an artificial reef by sinking large, hard objects for the mussels to attach themselves to. That's when New York City donated 400 retired . . .

___ ___ ___ ___ ___ ___   ___ ___ ___ ___

5 Deep Sea-crets

Now that highly developed modern submersibles can descend deeper than ever before, scientists are astounded by what they're finding in the sea.

Hard-Pressed: In the deep sea, it's vital to keep the weight of all that water from crushing the body. Without protective gear, air sacks in the lungs, ears, and nose would be crushed like a balloon squeezed between two strong hands—giving new meaning to the phrase "under pressure"! Without being inside a submersible, the deepest a human can go, even in a special diving outfit called a JIM suit, is 2,000 feet.

Fathom That!

The first submarine to be used in war was built in 1775 by David Bushnell and was called the . . .

a. *Sea Legend.*
b. *Dolphin.*
c. *Sea Serpent.*
d. *Turtle.*

Onward and Downward: Manned submarines can't go all the way to the deepest part of the ocean without being crushed to smithereens. In 1964, scientists built *Alvin,* a small submersible with very strong walls, that could take them as deep

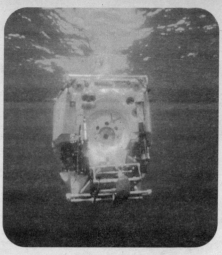

as 13,000 feet. Finally, scientists were able to look through *Alvin*'s portholes to view an underwater world never seen before!

Towering Infernos: In one spot on the ocean floor, tall towers rise up—more than 20 of them, like a gleaming city of underwater skyscrapers. The towers, called hydrothermal vents or black smokers, are found in several places in the ocean. They're formed when scalding water, laden with sulphur and other minerals and gases, bubbles up from deep inside the Earth and break through the ocean floor. When this super-hot stuff hits cold water, the minerals harden and the towers climb higher and higher.

Gas-tly Creatures: Scientists were astounded to find that billions of bacteria live in and around hydrothermal vents. How could these creatures survive without oxygen or sunlight? It turns out that the vents produce all they need: gases to feed on and warmth.

Gutless Wonders: Giant tubeworms also thrive near the vents. They have no eyes, mouths, or intestines. One end of the tube is attached to the seabed, and at the other end is a red plume used for breathing. The worms eat hydrogen sulfide gas that has been converted into nutrients by the bacteria that live inside their bodies.

Fathom That!

Scientists in submersibles have discovered black smokers as tall as . . .

a. 33 feet.
b. 230 feet.
c. 1,330 feet.
d. 2,033 feet.

Lights, Camera, Action! The *Titanic* was a huge luxury ocean liner that hit an iceberg on the very first trip it ever made in 1912. For more than half a century, divers longed to find the wreckage, but it lay way too deep—12,500 feet down on the floor of the north Atlantic. Once *Alvin* was built, marine explorers thought they might have a shot at finding the wreck. In 1985, explorers used *Alvin* and his two mechanical partners—*Jason* the robot and an underwater sled called *Argo,* which were steered by remote control and carried lights and video equipment to take panoramic and close-up shots.

Lost and Found: Late one night in September 1985, *Alvin*'s crew spied something interesting on the radar screen. Was it part of a ship? *Argo*'s pictures kept coming. More ship parts showed up. Could it be the *Titanic*?

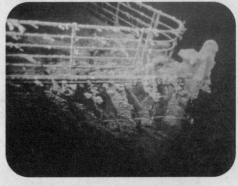

Jason was sent to get some close-ups—and the crew began to cheer! Yes! There were parts of the *Titanic*'s beautiful brass railing and elegant staircase, marble bathroom fixtures, and more! At last, the *Titanic* had been found.

How Iron-ic! Since the first discovery of the wreck of the *Titanic*, explorers have found other artifacts, including a gold pocket watch, a fancy purse, and a comb—all sad reminders of the passengers who once owned them. Today, divers continue to explore the ship, but they are running out of time. The wreck is being consumed by iron-eating underwater microbes called rusticules—at the rate of 200 pounds a day!

Taking the Plunge: A submersible is not needed to explore the Italian passenger ship, the *Andrea Doria*, whose wreckage lies just 225 feet below sea level about 50 miles south of Nantucket,

Massachusetts. Considered the Mount Everest of scuba diving, the ship is visited by divers from all over the world. Some divers hope to come away with a trophy—a teacup, a sterling silver fork, or even, in the case of one diver, a toilet for his new bathroom!

Fathom That!

In 1967, *Alvin* was attacked by a . . .

a. sperm whale and seriously damaged.
b. giant squid that pulled it like a sleigh for miles.
c. manatee that mistook it for a potential mate.
d. swordfish that got stuck in its gear and ended up as dinner for the crew.

Sunken City: Home to Cleopatra, one of the most beautiful and powerful queens who ever lived, the island of Antirhodos used to be located near the ancient Egyptian city of Alexandria. That was before floods and earthquakes caused the island to sink beneath the sea. Fast-forward to more than 1,600 years later: In 1996, marine explorer Frank Goddio and his crew discovered the ruins of what may have been Cleopatra's palace buried in mud just 18 feet underwater! After years of exploration, Goddio's crew found a royal treasure trove— including a statue of a sphinx. Half-human, half-lion, the statue has the face of King Ptolemy, Cleopatra's father!

Fathom That!

Considered to be one of the most precious artifacts ever recovered from a shipwreck, an astrolabe found in 1994 was used in the 1500s to . . .

a. tell time.
b. measure the height of waves.
c. calculate the position of the sun, moon, and stars.
d. detect the approach of pirates from afar.

Time Capsule:

To date, the oldest shipwreck ever found is the *Uluburun*. Discovered in 1984, the ship is thought to have sunk more than 3,000 years ago! Among the many

treasures archaeologists were delighted to find in the wreckage were early examples of wooden writing boards, ivory cosmetic containers, and a gold scarab inscribed with the name of Queen Nefertiti, who ruled Egypt during the 14th century BCE.

Brain Teaser:

In 1986, *La Belle*, a ship belonging to French explorer René-Robert La Salle (1643–1687), was discovered off the coast of Texas. As marine archaeologists went through the wreck, they found a lot more than they bargained for—tucked inside a big coil of rope was a skeleton! More impressive still was that the 300-year-old brain inside the skull was perfectly preserved! DNA tests were conclusive: The brain belonged to none other than La Salle himself.

Yo-ho-ho! In 1717, Blackbeard the Pirate captured a French slave-ship and used it to attack other ships off the coast of the British Colonies in America. In 1718, Blackbeard ran

the *Queen Anne's Revenge* aground off the coast of North Carolina. He abandoned the ship—and many of the crew—and made off with the loot. On November 21, 1996, following clues in old books and maps, Phil Masters of Intersal, a Florida-based salvage company, found an 18th-century wreck near Beaufort Inlet. It was the *Queen Anne's Revenge!* Since its discovery, more than 2,000 artifacts have been found, including 18 cannons and about 70 flakes of gold dust. What happened to Blackbeard? Six months after he abandoned ship, he was killed by Lieutenant Robert Maynard, who had Blackbeard's head cut off and hung from the bowsprit of his ship.

Fathom That!

The biggest annoyance to most marine archaeologists as they explore shipwrecks is . . .

a. freezing cold temperatures.
b. seaweed getting in the way.
c. fear of sharks.
d. curious octopuses that move things around.

Up, Up, and Away: How do archaeologists get the precious cargo they find beneath the sea up to the surface? They use airlifts and dredges that work like giant underwater vacuum

cleaners to remove the accumulations of sand and debris that often cover shipwrecks. Heavy items are floated to the surface by huge balloons called liftbags. The liftbags are filled with air from scuba tanks ever so slowly to control the speed at which the delicate cargo rises.

Life Preserver: What causes so much damage to wooden shipwrecks? Bacteria that eat the wood. Metal shipwrecks fall apart because they rust. Another word for rust is oxidation, which can't happen without oxygen. There's something really unusual about the Black Sea. Shipwrecks found there are very well preserved. Why?

The water there is full of hydrogen sulfide, which takes the place of oxygen—so metal doesn't rust and bacteria, most of which can't survive without oxygen, don't eat the wood. Believe It!

Jim Dandy! On September 19, 1979, Sylvia Earle descended as far below sea level as the Empire State Building rises above it—1,250 feet! A submersible took her to the seafloor, then she walked out on her own,

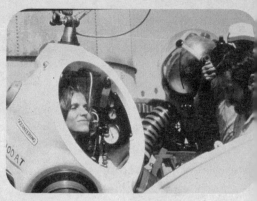

attached to the mother ship by a thick cable. Searle was wearing a JIM suit, named after Jim Jarrott, the first diver ever to wear it. The human-shaped suit with its heavy-duty walls gave her all the protection she needed.

Seeing the Light Show: Through the JIM suit's porthole, Sylvia Earle was treated to an extravagant light show. She touched a coral with her steel-gloved hand, and it responded to her with pulses of blue light. A lanternfish darted by, its sides dotted with lights like a mini ocean liner. Then a school of teeny fish swept past her face, flashing their lights like a swarm of fireflies.

Earle withdrew her hand within the cocoon of her JIM suit and took notes. When it was time to resurface, the crew contacted her by radio. Then they pulled her up like a puppet on a string.

Fathom That!

Divers can move fairly freely in the JIM suit because it has . . .

a. little oars attached to it.
b. a battery-operated propeller.
c. oil-filled ball-and-socket joints so divers can use their arms and legs.
d. a small outboard motor.

Reach for the Depths:

Engineers are constantly developing newer and better submersibles, designed to take researchers deeper and deeper into the ocean depths. A

vehicle called *Deep Flight* was designed to go very fast and handle like a sports car underwater. Newly designed submersibles will soon reach the deepest parts of the oceans. Getting there will be the closest thing to making an expedition to the center of Earth!

Seals of Approval:

Police in New York use a low-tech approach to sea exploration. Three seals, named Stanley, Raz, and Sirius, were specially trained at the North Wind Undersea Institute on City Island in New York City to assist the police and coast guard in rescue missions and in finding objects underwater.

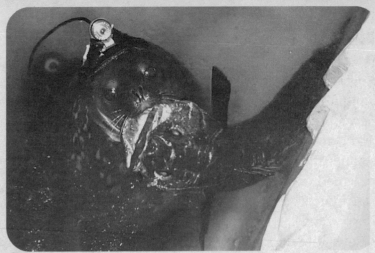

Critter-cal Care: Marine biologists have always wondered how sea creatures behave when no one is around to observe them. One day, marine biologist Greg Marshall saw a shark swim by with a smaller fish suction-cupped to its body. Why not substitute a video camera for the fish? he wondered. It wasn't long before Crittercam was born. The camera can be easily attached to sea turtles, seals, and other sea creatures to allow scientists to see what they do from the animal's point of view. One result of Crittercam research is that we now know that monk seals hunt for food a lot farther out in the ocean than once thought. That knowledge makes it possible for authorities to protect this endangered species more effectively.

Fathom That!

Originally the size of a coffee can, newly designed Crittercam models can be as small as a . . .

a. deck of cards.
b. cell phone.
c. marker pen.
d. soda can.

Though deep-sea exploration can more often than not seem like science fiction, three of the following statements are deeply true. Can you spot the one that doesn't even skim the surface?

a. Scientists can use sonar to send sound waves to the ocean floor. The longer it takes for the echo to bounce up, the deeper the water.

b. Daniel D. Lung, the first marine researcher to descend to 1,500 feet, pedaled his way down in a deep-sea vessel called the Aquacycle.

c. In 1934, Charles Beebe was lowered in a soccer ball–shaped vessel called the bathyscaphe to a depth of 3,028 feet.

d. A 24,000-mile-long chain of underwater volcanoes in the Pacific Ocean is called the Ring of Fire.

BONUS GAME

Naval scientist Bruce Denardo forced air bubbles underneath balls in a beaker of water, causing the balls to sink. Perhaps, he concluded, water that's aerated by gases bubbling up from the ocean floor is not heavy enough to support ships. Perhaps this is the real explanation of why so many ships have mysteriously disappeared in the area known as the . . .

_ _ _ _ _ _ _   _ _ _ _ _ _ _

POP QUIZ

Still got your sea legs? Good! It's time to reach deep down into your vast ocean of knowledge and find out if you remember enough weird and mysterious facts about the sea to make a big splash with your Ripley's score!

1. The seafloor is full of . . .
a. mountains.
b. caves.
c. valleys.
d. all of the above.

2. The deepest parts of the ocean are called . . .
a. salt cellars.
b. sea pits.
c. marine ravines.
d. trenches.

3. In August 2000, the citizens of Great Yarmouth, England, were astonished to discover that a waterspout had covered their lawns with . . .
a. fish.
b. tadpoles.
c. thousands of marbles.
d. toads.

4. An adult blue whale can weigh as much as . . .

a. a barrel full of monkeys.

b. 30 full-grown elephants.

c. a school bus full of high-school students.

d. an army tank.

5. No one has ever captured a giant squid.

Believe It!   **Not!**

6. Cuttlefish use color changes as . . .

a. camouflage.

b. to attract a mate.

c. hypnotize prey.

d. all of the above.

7. Fish traveling in schools seem to move as one fish because their bodies are equipped with . . .

a. blinking directional signals similar to those on a car.

b. sensors that detect even the tiniest vibrations in water.

c. underwater sound systems.

d. skin that changes color to communicate direction.

8. Coral will attach itself to . . .

a. skeletons of fish.

b. rocks.

c. shipwrecks.

d. all of the above.

9. The only fish immune to anemone stings are . . .
a. clownfish.
b. wrasse.
c. triggerfish.
d. sharks.

10. A waxy gray substance found in the large intestines of sperm whales is used as a base used to make expensive perfumes.

Believe It!   **Not!**

11. Carrageenan, an ingredient in many foods such as ice cream, is derived from . . .
a. seaweed.
b. sea slugs.
c. oysters.
d. manta rays.

12. Scientists have discovered anti-viral compounds to fight diseases like malaria in . . .
a. clam shells.
b. mussels.
c. deep-sea sponges.
d. coral.

13. Deep-sea explorers wear special gear to protect themselves from the effects of . . .
a. salt water.
b. extreme water pressure.
c. octopus ink.
d. sand abrasions.

14. While exploring the shipwreck of the *LaBelle*, divers came across a map leading to buried treasure.

Believe It!   **Not!**

15. In 1996, marine explorer Frank Goddio discovered the ruins of what might have been . . .
a. the lost city of Atlantis.
b. the ruins of Troy.
c. Julius Caesar's tomb.
d. Cleopatra's palace.

Answer Key

Chapter 1
Way Down Under
Page 5:   **c.** six feet.
Page 6:   **d.** the mounds that tilefish build to hide themselves from predators.
Page 9:   **c.** smaller.
Page 10   **b.** thick, abundant, floating seaweed.
Page 13:   **d.** three miles.
Page 15:   **a.** shallowest ocean.
Page 17:   **c.** 1,720 feet high.
Page 18:   **d.** live toads.
Brain Buster: c. is false.
Bonus Game: 1=d, 2=c, 3=b, 4=a

Chapter 2
Supersized!
Page 21:   **b.** compact car.
Page 23:   **d.** once an hour.
Page 25:   **a.** travel around the entire Earth.
Page 27:   **c.** money.
Page 29:   **a.** are very social animals that usually travel in pods.
Page 31:   **b.** eyelids.
Page 33:   **c.** hundred million eggs.
Page 34:   **a.** for sandpaper.
Brain Buster: d. is false.
Bonus Game: Giant barrel sponge

Chapter 3
Sea-riously Strange!

Page 37: **d.** by drilling a hole in the clam's shell with its tongue.

Page 39: **c.** that is twice their size.

Page 40: **b.** light-emitting organs.

Page 42: **a.** hitches a ride on a parrotfish.

Page 44: **c.** pushes the salp around like a baby carriage until the young have hatched.

Page 47: **c.** water.

Page 48: **a.** releasing a cloud of glowing, bioluminescent ink to blind them.

Brain Buster: a. is false.

Bonus Game: Sea serpents

Chapter 4
Gifts from the Sea

Page 51: **a.** boots.

Page 53: **a.** nasal spray for allergy sufferers.

Page 54: **c.** rare, bright orange pearls.

Page 57: **d.** diamonds.

Page 58: **c.** test medicine for bacteria.

Brain Buster: b. is false.

Bonus Game: Subway cars

Chapter 5
Deep Sea-crets

Page 61:   **d.** *Turtle.*

Page 63:   **a.** 33 feet.

Page 65:   **d.** swordfish that got stuck in its gear and ended up as dinner for the crew.

Page 66:   **c.** calculate the position of the sun, moon, and stars.

Page 68:   **d.** curious octopuses that move things around.

Page 70:   **c.** oil-filled ball-and-socket joints so divers can use their arms and legs.

Page 72:   **c.** marker pen.

Brain Buster: **b.** is false.

Bonus Game: Bermuda Triangle

Pop Quiz

1. **d.**
2. **d.**
3. **a.**
4. **b.**
5. **Believe It!**
6. **d.**
7. **b.**
8. **d.**
9. **a.**
10. **Believe It!**
11. **a.**
12. **c.**
13. **b.**
14. **Not!**
15. **d.**

What's Your Ripley's Rank?

Ripley's Scorecard

Congratulations! You've busted your brain over some of the wildest and wackiest sea-crets and proven your ability to tell fact from fiction. Now it's time to rate your Ripley's knowledge. Are you are a **Landlubber** or a **Sea Star**? Check out the answer key and use this page to keep track of how many trivia questions you've answered correctly. Then add them up and find out how you rate.

Here's the scoring breakdown. Give yourself:
★ **10 points** for every **Fathom That!** you answered correctly;
★ **20 points** for every fiction you spotted in the **Ripley's Brain Busters**;
★ **10 points** every time you solved a **Bonus Game**;
★ and **5 points** for every **Pop Quiz** question you got right.

Here's a tally sheet:
Number of **Fathom That!**
questions answered correctly: _____ x 10 = _____
Number of **Ripley's Brain Buster**
fictions spotted: _____ x 20 = _____
Number of **Bonus Games**
questions you solved: _____ x 10 = _____
Number of **Pop Quiz** questions
answered correctly: _____ x 5 = _____

Total the right column for your final score: _____

0–100
Landlubber

Does your score make you feel like you're drowning in a sea of strange information? Don't worry. Maybe the ocean and its many weird creatures just aren't your thing. Perhaps you prefer reading about animals that live on land. No problem. There are lots of other Ripley's Believe It or Not! books to try. Check out *Awesome Animals, Bizarre Bugs,* or *Weird Pet Stories.* You're sure to find something you'll be able to plunge right into.

101–250
Sea Squirt

Okay, so you didn't earn the highest score, but you didn't do too badly, either. It's obvious that you're beginning to learn how to swim through the kind of weird and wacky sea stories that are found in this book. Keep diving for clues, and you'll soon be up to your gills in amazing sea trivia!

251–400
Swellshark

Wow! You really took a bite out of these tests! Your high score proves that you have a sea-rious attention span and a fin-tastic memory to boot. Keep up the good work and with just a little more practice, you'll soon make it to the top of the Ripley's scorecard.

401–575
Sea Star

Congratulations! You've earned yourself a whale of a score and made a big splash! Robert Ripley would be proud of you. Your knack for soaking up bizarre sea mysteries is truly awesome. Now that you've soaked up *Mysteries of the Sea,* you're probably ready to come up for air and read strange and unusual facts on other subjects. Well, you won't have to hold your breath for long. More new Ripley's Believe It or Not! books will be coming your way soon!

Believe It!®

Photo Credits

Ripley Entertainment Inc. and the editors of this book wish to thank the following photographers, agents, and other individuals for permission to use and reprint the following photographs in this book. Any photographs included in this book that are not acknowledged below are property of the Ripley Archives. Great effort has been made to obtain permission from the owners of all materials included in this book. Any errors that may have been made are unintentional and will gladly be corrected in future printings if notice is sent to Ripley Entertainment Inc., 7576 Kingspointe Parkway, Suite 188, Orlando, Florida 32819.

Black & White Photos

7   Great Rift Valley/Getty Images/ Joseph Van Os

9   Caribbean Reef Shark, 11 Diver in Kelp Forest, 28 Cuttlefish, 38 School of Fish, 41 Coral on Airplane Wreck, 42 Parrotfish, 45 Starfish, 47 Hawksbill Turtle, 48 Red Gilled Nudibranch/Corel

12 Bioluminescing Firefly Squid/Y Kito/Image Quest Marine 3-D

14 Tripod Fish, 38 Gulper Eel/Natural Visions/Peter David

21 Blue Whale/Getty Images/Taxi

22 Whale Breaching/Getty Images/Brand X Pictures/Brakefield Photo

24 Humpback Whale, 29 Great White Shark, 30 Whale Shark, 31 Hammerhead Shark, 32 Crown of Thorns Starfish, 39 Leafy Seadragon, 43 Wrasse and Coral Trout/ CORBIS

24 Sperm Whales/AP Photo/Guam Variety News/Chris Bangs

26 Giant Squid/Reuters/HO

30 Great White Shark/Getty Images/Image Bank/Amos Nachoum

52 Perfume Bottles/Getty Images/ Photodisc/Steve Cole

55 Mussels/Natural Visions

57 Deep-sea Oarfish/Seapics/Jonathan Bird

61 WASP version of JIM suit, 62 Alvin, 62 Black Smoker, 70 Sylvia Earle/OAR/National Undersea Research Program (NURP)

64 Titanic Wreckage/AP Photo/Nauticus

66 Diver and Sphinx, 71 Deep Flight/ Newscom/HO

69 Liftbags/Newscom/Paul Miller

72 Monk Seal Wearing Crittercam/AP Photo/Texas A&M University

Color Insert

(1) Coelacanth/Seapics/Mark V. Erdmann; Goblin Shark/Seapics/David Shen; Chambered Nautilis/Corel

(2-3) Mimic Octopus/Seapics; Clownfish, Fire Urchin, Porcupine Fish, Cuttlefish, Sand Diver Lizardfish/Corel

(4-5) Flashlight Fish, Jellyfish/Seapics/Shedd Aquar; Lycoteuthis Squid/Peter Parks/Image Quest Marine 3-D; Anglerfish, Viperfish and Shrimp/Edith Widder/HBOI; Stoplight Loosejaw Fish/Image Quest Marine 3-D

(6-7) Fairy Basslet, Jeweled-top Snail, Tubastraea Coral, Red-spotted Blenny, Wolf Eel/Corel; Batfish/OAR/National Undersea Research Program (NURP)

(8) Alvin, Black Smoker, Tubeworms/ OAR/ National Undersea Research Program (NURP)

Cover

Shipwreck/CORBIS; Viperfish/HBOI; Seahorse, Purple Nudibranch/Corel

Don't miss these  **Ripley's Believe It or Not!** other exciting books . . .

World's Weirdest Critters

Creepy Stuff

Odd-inary People

Amazing Escapes

World's Weirdest Gadgets

Bizarre Bugs

Blasts from the Past

Awesome Animals

Weird Science

X-traordinary X-tremes

Strange School Stories

Weird Pet Stories

Top 10: The Weirdest of the Weird

WE'D LOVE TO BELIEVE
YOU!

Do you have a Believe It or Not!
story that has happened to you or to
someone you know? If it's strange enough
and if you would like to share it, the people at
Ripley's would love to hear about it. You can
send your Believe It or Not! entries to:

**The Director of the Archives
Ripley Entertainment Inc.
7576 Kingspointe Parkway,
Suite 188
Orlando, Florida 32819**

Believe It!®